POWER TOOLS FOR LEADERSHIP SUCCESS

KATHERINE CRAIG

Power Tools For Leadership Success

Power Tools For Leadership Success

Katherine Craig

Illustrations by Emma Vaughan.

First published by Dog Ear Publishing
4010 W. 86th Street, Ste H
Indianapolis, IN 46268
www.dogearpublishing.net

ISBN: 978-1-4575-1110-3

This book is printed on acid-free paper.

Printed in the United States of America

TABLE OF CONTENTS

TEN

ACKNOWLEDGEMENTS

I owe a big part of this book, and my work, to my parents. They instilled in me both a disciplined work ethic and an unfailing desire to help others succeed. They taught me how to get up when I was down, and they always believed in my ability to get up, no matter how far down I might be.

To my family, Michael, Jessie and Paul, where would I be without you? You are the rock that grounds me. You have been unfailingly supportive in the development of this book. A special thanks to Jessie for all her extra help during her own difficult times. It takes a special person to help others when you are already taxed to the max.

I continue to appreciate Sara Lynn Grady, who was key to every aspect of this book. I couldn't have done it without her! She is the humor when I am discouraged and she helps me look to the horizon when I'm stuck looking at my toes.

To my friend and colleague, Kathy Austin, thank you for so generously sharing your time and expertise. Your editorial support was invaluable.

Finally, thanks to all the people—clients and friends—who shared their thoughts and insights in the development of this book. Their comments at coaching sessions, speaking engagements and workshops guide me. As ever, help is a two-way street!

FOREWORD

I was coaching a new client one morning, working through the list of goals and strategies we'd been exploring in our session, when he suddenly blurted out, "I just want all the tips at once! Can't I just have them all at once?!"

While there isn't a "magic wand" or shortcut to great leadership, there are some straightforward steps you can take *right now* that will change the way you lead your team. That's what you'll find here: simple, yet powerful, tools that will make you a better leader.

As my clients will attest, these aren't the only tools; they represent the beginnings of building your strength as a leader, and by using them as part of your daily, deliberate effort, you will see immediate results.

Power Tools—
Turning Thought into Action

How many of us have gone to a conference, heard a speaker, or read about an idea that really fired our engine, only to have the inspiration fade away over time? We have every intention of implementing a new plan and changing our leadership strategy, but we get sucked back into the tornado of day-to-day operations, and the ideas blow away. Sometimes, we just don't know how to begin to turn a concept into action.

That's what this book is all about. At the beginning of each section, I'll introduce a new concept that has been shown time and again to impact our ability to lead effectively. At the end of each chapter you'll find the **Power Tools.** *These are the concrete actions you can take to build your leadership skills.*

If you master these tools, you've got a great beginning to great leadership. It may sound easy, but it can be extremely difficult. Your work environment may be surprisingly resistant to what seems to you like a brilliant idea. What separates a great leader from all the good leaders out there is the ability to turn thought into action over and over again. In other words, great leadership takes practice.

Be persistent in your pursuit to be a great leader! Constantly move from thought to action, and take your leadership—and your team—from good to great!

But First, the Blueprints

In the pages that follow, I'll be sharing specific tools I've developed based on my 20 years of experience as an executive coach and mentor. These ideas didn't come to me overnight: I've been able to build and refine them over time by maintaining a structure, or blueprint, that guides my progress. I strongly urge you to try this for yourself and give shape to your ideas, as well.

1. **Keep a notebook handy** (electronic or otherwise). You have great ideas. When they come to you (mine happen immediately upon waking, so the notebook stays on my bedside table), you can write them down. Write them down as soon as you think of them.

2. **Review your ideas**, at least once a week. You may find that the ideas follow a theme. Ask yourself these questions: Why did I think of this idea? Was it a solution to a problem? Is it a method to "freshen up" a stale operation? How can I apply this idea?

3. **Put rigor to your ideas.** What resources will it take to try the idea out? How could I make this work? Your brain may have been tussling with a problem without you even being fully aware! Articulate the thought so that you can easily talk about it. Our brains do a funny trick of not being in partnership with our mouths when it's time to share our ideas with peers or our boss. Say your idea out loud until it's on the tip of your tongue and fluent.

4. **Sketch out an implementation plan.** Often it's wise to try the idea on a smaller scale before you go whole hog. I love the concept of a "test drive" approach. It gives everyone a chance to try the car before buying it. Think about seeding some champions around you. They are often the difference between implementation success and failure. Not familiar with seeding champions? Seeding champions refers to the practice of creating a core group of people who will help carry your idea across the organization. You can't be in every discussion around every corner, but your champions can be, and they'll carry your message in

the positive fashion you desire. The more champions, the better!

5. **Act!** Get out of your chair and carry out your implementation plan. **Set some time aside in your calendar and do it...now.**

ONE

Gather Feedback ... From Unlikely Sources

"Drowning in data yet starved of information."

—Ruth Stanat

LEADERS NEED INFORMATION. It fuels evaluation, closes the loop on projects and provides a measuring stick for future success. You're going to receive updates and reports from your boss, your peers, and your team, but there are other sources of information that can throw a light into the corners you wouldn't necessarily see with the standard reports and feedback. Here are four great sources of alternative information:

✓ Cab drivers

✓ Cafe cashiers

✓ Cleaning staff

✓ Administrative support staff

Want to know what people are saying about your company "on the street"? Ask a cab driver. So many folks forget they're not alone in a taxi and have surprisingly candid conversations with a fellow passenger or on their mobile. If you're in the midst of a massive layoff or about to launch a new product, chances are your cabbie has caught wind and will have some interesting insights to share. A simple question like, "What have you heard around town about the job losses at (your company)?" can launch a revealing discussion about the outside image of your inner workings.

Cashiers in the cafeteria are also part of the invisible staff. I've witnessed firsthand a shockingly candid discussion between two senior executives standing across the counter from a cafeteria cashier, who quickly realized she was overhearing some highly sensitive details about the department down the hall. Again, a very straightforward question can lead to some illuminating answers. "I hear they're reorganizing a couple of departments later this month, what's the buzz down here?"

This same principle applies to cleaning staff. In fact, I know one highly successful senior executive who deliberately stays late to talk to the janitors on his floor. We tend to filter out our surroundings when having a "confidential" conversation and forget that we're not alone. These invisible employees hear a great deal in the course of their day, and chances are, they interact with everyone from the junior staffers in the mailroom right up to the executives in the C-suite (the CEO, CFO, COO).

Finally, your last golden source of feedback is the administrative support staff. They tend to be the constant in a highly fluid executive atmosphere. As the gatekeepers, glue and band-aids in a given department, their insight and observations are extremely valuable. Tread carefully, though; asking the wrong question can put them in a compromising position. You're looking for their opinions, not facts that might be confidential in nature. It's okay to ask, "What do you think about that shuffle they're doing in Marketing this month?" It's a no-no to say, "You've got the inside track, what's your bosses' position on that shuffle they're doing in Marketing this month?"

Be the leader. Gather feedback. Gather perspectives.

Power Tools

Open Sesame!

People often say to me, "I've got someone in mind to speak with but don't know what to ask." Here are some questions to get you going. Remember to let the source talk—this isn't the time to argue your case! You are there gathering information.

Are you familiar with (your company)?

Are you familiar with (this issue)?

What do you know about (the company/issue)?

What rumors have you heard?

What do you think (your company) is doing right/ wrong?

What would you like to see happen?

TWO

Make Meetings Matter

"The good news is that there is nothing inherent about meetings that makes them bad, and so it is entirely possible to transform them into compelling, productive and fun activities."

—Patrick Lencioni

ALL TOO OFTEN I hear the complaint about "meeting bloat"—that tedious habit of calling a meeting on every issue. We've all had a boss or project lead who loves to call meetings. Their purpose? Nobody ever really knows. Participants read status reports that could have been e-mailed, describing things that have already happened that don't benefit from your input, or anyone else's in the room, for that matter. Nailed to your chair, you spend the meeting thinking about how much you could have accomplished in the hour you've spent spinning your tires, and your frustration level increases tenfold.

Meetings should never be about status reports. Ever. **Meetings should be about getting a group of people together to push action forward.** But how do you transform your meetings from a day stuck in the mud to a day that feels really worthwhile?

First, let's take a look at the different types of meetings you and your team will need*:

---

*Check out *Death by Meeting* by Paul Lencioni for great meeting tips. See Recommended Reading for details.

Daily Check-up. Dedicate 10 minutes at the beginning of each day to do a quick ground-level check-up: Does everybody have the tools and resources they need to get through the day? Think of rounds in a hospital or shift change at a nursing station. There isn't a formal agenda; this is just an opportunity to help ensure everybody is on track for the day. (It has been my experience that these types of meetings work best when the team is collocated rather than geographically dispersed. Different time zones can throw a real monkey wrench into schedules.)

Weekly Tactical. Take a half hour (one hour, max) to do an assessment of immediate and short-term project needs. Think of this as the view from 5000 feet. This isn't a time for strategizing; this is a time to go around the room and establish what resources are needed and what decisions have to be made for a successful week. You're going to build the agenda in the first five minutes of the meeting based on a "lightning round"—participants will answer the question "What has to be decided today for you to proceed this week?" Your agenda will be a list of decisions or action items. At the end of the meeting, these items will result in tangible activities that advance the project and/or the team.

Monthly Meeting. From 20,000 feet, the participants in the room will be able to see the big picture. This is a time to strategize and set long-term visions, goals and objectives. The agenda will be set and will have a maximum of three topics to be explored. You'll need a few hours and only high-level leaders in the room.

Quarterly Retreat. No, I'm not talking about a boozy golf tournament and monotone speeches. Retreats are an incredibly powerful tool, one you can use to build four strong pillars for short- and long-term growth. Here are your four pillars:

✓ Learning and Skills Development

✓ Strategy Sessions

✓ Team Building and Networking

✓ Reflection on Successes

An effective retreat can be held during business hours so you're not running into extra expense. Even two per year will give your team opportunities to learn about the company's vision and your vision, and provide a forum to share insights you might not hear from them day to day. This is especially important for infrastructure groups such as HR or Finance that are collocated with the teams they support. Regular retreats connect these groups back to their coworkers and reestablish departmental priorities. (More about retreats in Chapter Seven.)

Recently, I had a client tell me that she finally decided to overhaul her meetings. In the new format she began with each person sharing a work success, moved to a lightning round to strike an agenda of immediate issues requiring team input, then used that agenda to guide the meeting. Commitments were summarized for future reference.

She offered words of encouragement and asked for input. Otherwise, she remained (relatively) quiet. She reported that the meeting, which in previous months had been filled with silence and fidgeting, was instead full of lively discussion where everyone participated. At the end of the meeting the team unanimously voted to keep the new format. People actually reported being excited about the meeting!

Be the leader. Take action. Make meetings matter.

Power Tools

Think Before You Book

- ✓ **Question the need.** Do you really need the whole team in the room or will a five-minute one-on-one with a member of your department do the trick?

- ✓ **Have an agenda of decisions to be made.**

- ✓ **Get the right people in the room.** Resist the urge to invite the entire department! The purpose of a meeting is to push action forward, so take a moment to consider who you need and who you don't. Will your team benefit from outside information or support?

- ✓ **Schedule guests for a specific time on your agenda.** This will give your meeting focus and ensure your guests are willing to return.

Mix It Up (and Other Quick Tips)

- ✓ **Start at an odd time.** Switching up the start time is like throwing Turkish dates in your oatmeal instead of California raisins. Mixing it up is good.

- ✓ **Keep it short.** Brevity really is bliss. Don't let anyone tell you otherwise.

- ✓ **Listen, really listen.** Challenge yourself to listen without intent to respond. You'll be surprised what you hear.

- ✓ **Build a virtual parking lot** to hold ideas you want to deal with later. The lightning round will generate issues you'll need to revisit at a later date.

Put these ideas in the parking lot, and remember the stall number.

✓ **Standing room only.** We've been reading about the dangers of sitting too much on the job. Why not make your weekly meetings a stand-up affair?

✓ **Eliminate e-traffic.** If your meetings are short, concise and action-based, e-mail surfing under the table won't be a temptation. Just to be sure, ban the handheld and keep everyone focussed.

✓ **Be consistent.** Pick a few meeting strategies and stick with them.

Improve Your Style

Some leaders are natural public speakers and guide a room through an agenda with ease and clarity. That's a rare quality, though. More often than not, that seemingly natural leader has taken the time to study the art of conducting meetings. There is an abundance of information, whether you hit the bookstore, hit the Internet or join a professional association. Here are a few common issues you might be facing, along with a couple of sources and tips to get you going.

Issue: You lack confidence, have poor presentation skills.

Source: Toastmasters have the solution for this down to a science. I have seen them take poor speakers and give them the confidence and polish to really shine at the front of a room. They seem to be in most every town, so it's worth it to investigate. The bottom line is always: practice, practice, practice!

Issue: You ramble.

Tip: Before you start to speak...prepare! If you only have moments to prepare, jot down two or three key points to gather your thoughts. You are likely rambling as a means to sort out your thoughts. People don't want to hear your cogitations and will likely tune out when you start to speak. You might be perceived as lacking in vision and decisiveness. Be crisp with your key points. Practice doing this to gain speed.

If you require more time to provide an intelligent answer to a question, by all means say so, using phrases like "This sounds interesting—I'd like to look at it more thoroughly and will get back to you by the end of the day/by tomorrow/by the end of the week" or "While this all looks in order, there's something that doesn't feel quite right. Let me look over it again and get back to you by the end of the day/by tomorrow/by the end of the week." (Did you notice that in the two responses there is a clear time when you will provide the feedback? This is important. Decisiveness isn't about answering **now**, it's about having a plan of action.)

Issue: You are too crisp and brief.

Do you feel somewhat isolated at work? Do you have trouble warming to people? Is time always short? Are meetings just a tool to get the job done? If you are the leader, are you able to speak with members of your team about non-work issues? Do you find the last question ridiculous?

Tip: Your first line of action to consider would be retaining the services of a business coach to help you reframe your workplace and connect to your team. You are not alone in this! I coach many leaders with this challenge. It's likely you have skills to deal with this issue and simply aren't applying them to the workplace.

You're right; time is short and workloads are huge. To that point, make sure your meetings are (a) necessary (not used for status updates that could be mailed) and (b) structured properly. If those two components are in place, then you are on the right path. Lastly, take a few minutes before/during/after a meeting to show your team a "personal" side and a bit of what makes you interested and interesting. If they don't know you, it's difficult to follow you as a leader. This will warm your cool-and-brisk persona.

THREE

Keep Your Boss Informed

"Communication works for those who work at it."

—John Powell

AS A LEADER, you tend to focus on managing the people you're leading. But you also need to manage the people leading you. You need to manage upwards. We all have bosses, whether we're the division manager or the CFO. And these bosses need to know what we're doing.

So consider this. It's time for your annual performance review. Your boss informs you that you'll be writing it for him (again) and he'd like it by week's end. You wonder, Is my boss lazy, or does he simply have no clue what I do all day?

Okay, there are some leaders out there who don't attack their jobs with the vigor one might find inspiring, but the odds are better that your superior genuinely doesn't know about your daily successes and challenges. And how could he if you don't tell him?

As I mentioned before, leaders need information. Providing your boss with regular status updates will serve myriad purposes, not the least of which is making your annual review just that, a *review* of your status updates.

This is particularly helpful if your boss lives in another city or country. Her only source of information might be quantitative statistics and secondhand reports unless you provide her with more detailed information.

What are the elements of a good update?

✓ Targets

✓ Performance

✓ Timing

Your updates should answer these questions to keep your leader in the loop:

✓ What are your short- and long-term targets?

✓ Have you achieved these targets?

✓ Was this ahead of, behind, or on schedule?

✓ When do you anticipate completion of pending projects?

✓ What resources do you need to finish those projects?

I know, you don't think you have time to write another report. You don't have to. In fact, you really shouldn't.

This isn't a diary, so bullets are fine. All you need is a running account of your activities. It might take some time to get into a rhythm, but these updates should take 15 minutes to write and five minutes to read. Just think of the time you'll save down the road when it's time to write your performance review! And that's not the only perk.

✓ Want to settle a dispute over where or when a project stalled? Pull out your updates and find the entry citing a breakdown in the system.

✓ Want to recognize individuals on your team at the annual retreat with concrete examples of their achievements? Pull out your updates and find the entries detailing their contributions.

✓ Taking time to evaluate yourself and your accomplishments? Pull out your updates and see if you're meeting your personal targets. (I'll talk later about self-reflection, where these updates can serve a purpose when looking back to plan your next steps moving forward.)

✓ Finding that one-on-one meetings with your boss are consumed with merely catching up, leaving no time to discuss anything else? Your monthly updates will put key issues at the top of your valuable meetings!

Be the leader. Track your progress. Share successes.

Power Tools

Often, people can't get out of the gate on this particular action because they have trouble figuring out what kind of format to use. There are so many options, a phenomenon called "choice anxiety" comes into play. Don't worry about whether you have the perfect chart! Focus on what you really need: a vehicle that will keep your boss informed and also serve as a platform for your successes.

To that end, think of these words:

✓ Simple

✓ Clean

✓ User-friendly

✓ Quick to read

As mentioned in the chapter, your boss doesn't want to read a diary. Your boss wants an at-a-glance update. Your update should reflect that and serve both of you.

If the core components of target, performance and timing are there, it should do the trick. Whether your report is in the form of bullets or a Gantt-type chart is a matter of preference. Once you have the first one completed and sent along, take a few minutes alone with your boss and ask if the format was useful. Ask the following questions:

✓ Was this useful to you?

✓ Was it easy to read?

✓ Are there any formatting changes you'd like to see that would put the information more clearly at your fingertips?

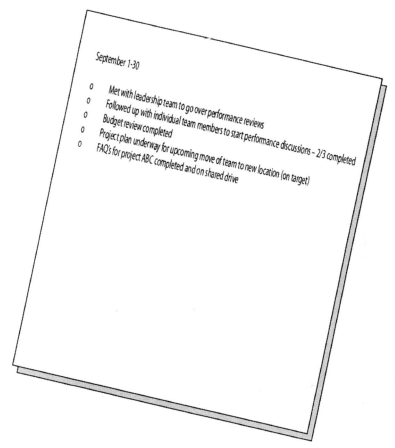

September 1-30

o   Met with leadership team to go over performance reviews
o   Followed up with individual team members to start performance discussions – 2/3 completed
o   Budget review completed
o   Project plan underway for upcoming move of team to new location (on target)
o   FAQ's for project ABC completed and on shared drive

Example of a Monthly Report in Word

FOUR

Manage Technology
(Don't Let Technology Manage You)

"Everybody gets so much information all day long that they lose their common sense."

— Gertrude Stein

THIS SHOULD BE common sense; alas, I see it often enough that it warrants a place on the top-10 list. Here's what happens: in lower management, the job is framed by "tasks" requiring action; the volume of phone calls and e-mails is considerable, and they often need immediate attention to keep projects moving forward.

As you work your way up the ladder, though, people start working for you, carrying out those action tasks based on the strategies you've set. In the C-suite, your job has become one of setting vision and leading planning for short- and long-term goals, and then guiding your team as they set about achieving the goals with your support.

The cell phone is still a tether, though, a force of habit. So when one of your team leaders asks for a face-to-face regarding a sensitive issue, there it sits on your desk, buzzing away as you surreptitiously glance to see who's calling or e-mailing.*

---

*If your boss is driving the "be at my beck and call" issue, it's time for a careful conversation with him about the message you are sending people when you compulsively check your phone like you've been touched by a cattle prod. Does he really expect you to drop everything to answer his call, or is that just your misguided perception? There may be times in the pursuit of good leadership that you turn off the phone to give a face-to-face conversation your full attention. Beg forgiveness from the boss later.

You think you're being discreet and still giving your attention to the person sitting across the desk explaining that she's about to undergo a medical procedure and needs a leave of absence, but she knows she only has half your attention at best. The anxiety she's feeling about her operation, not to mention the disruption it will cause in her department, is magnified by the lack of concern you're showing her. As a leader, you are failing her.

We talk a lot about discipline throughout the book. As a leader, you need to exercise discipline when it comes to your interactions with technology. Don't let technology define your leadership style. Use the time-saving tools available to enhance your ability to interact with your team, not to take you away.

Be the leader. Pay attention. Manage technology.

Power Tools

Issue: You can't help yourself—it really is a Crackberry!

The first course of action is to identify why you think you can't turn it off—awareness will set you free. Is it because you love technology and the instant gratification it promises? Is it because you are afraid you will miss something? Will your boss tear your arm off and beat you with the wet end if you miss her call?

If your answer is yes to any variety of the first two reasons, then it's time to prioritize. Now's the time to focus.

If someone on your team has asked for "time alone" to speak with you about an important issue, take the following steps:

1. Welcome her in and tell her she is important and that you want a moment to turn everything off so your meeting won't be interrupted.

2. Turn your computer screen off.

3. Turn your cell phone completely off and put it in a drawer.

4. Put the phone on your desk to call messaging (it's one button!).

5. Now listen, really listen.

Issue: You have no time…for anything.

There are plenty of time-saving tips on the Internet. Try some out and keep using the ideas that work for you. Here are a few of them:

✓ **Block time to work on e-mails.** Mentally address them in three categories: easy and quick to address, medium and will take a couple of minutes, hard and will take a fair amount of time. Blast through the easy e-mails at regular times in the day when you have 10 minutes or so. The medium and hard e-mails should be addressed with the door shut when you won't be interrupted. Turn your phone off so you can work through them smoothly and efficiently.

✓ **Pick up the phone.** If an issue is taking more than four or five e-mails to resolve, then make a call. E-mail trails are notorious time suckers and can make you crazy.

✓ **Delete the cc's.** I know one leader who deletes e-mails that she is cc'd on. She believes if it's something she really needs to know, then it will be sent to her directly. This is pretty drastic, I know, but you could just wait for a long time to open them or throw them in a file for later reference.

✓ **Delete the obsolete.** If you have e-mails that have been in your inbox for longer than three or four months, ditch them. They are obsolete. If the issue was that serious, the person would already have put a price on your head for not answering sooner.

✓ **Keep it short.** Make your e-mails incredibly short and demand that others do the same when writing you. E-mails are not meant to be letters; they are meant to be messages. Write exactly what is needed—bulleted comments can be your friend.

✓ **Battle the backlog.** The leaders I know who are really effective have no more e-mails in their inbox than are visible on one screen. That's less than 50. You can do it. It's all about getting on top of that crazy backlog of mail and staying there.

✓ **Don't ramble.** Do you get long-winded voice-mail messages? Worse yet, are you the author of these narratives? I heard one executive say that at the 30-second mark, she deletes the message. Keep your messages short and to the point. It's not a conversation; it's a message.

FIVE

Put the Rumor Mill in Its Place

"Understanding human needs is half the job of meeting them."

— Adlai Stevenson

WE'VE TALKED ABOUT the importance of getting information from unlikely sources and of sharing information that highlights your successes. Now we're going to talk about handling information that addresses corporate crises.

Crisis is a universal condition, no matter the size or composition of your company. Whether it's an internal issue like the sudden firing or resignation of a key staffer or an external issue like a downturn in the economy that makes your organization vulnerable, you will have to address situations that throw your company into a state of crisis.

It's important to know that the crisis itself isn't the biggest issue you have to address with your staff; it's the time span between finding out there is a crisis and learning what's going to be done about it that you need to keep on your radar.

Nature abhors a vacuum. If you don't provide information, people will listen to the rumor mill, whether that information is accurate or not. Hearing about your company's crisis in the news, or from the neighbor, creates an internal crisis. Your star employees will start job hunting unless they get a rebuttal (or confirmation) from you.

You can't avoid corporate crisis, but you can avoid the catastrophic effects it can have on your team.

✓ **Be visible!** Don't hide or shut your office door when the fertilizer hits the fan. Delay your vacation if you have to; just don't be absent when news of the crisis starts to circulate.

✓ **Tell them what you know.** Don't know anything yet? *Tell them* you don't know anything yet. Is head office trying to sort things out? Tell them that. Is the next step planned but still confidential? Tell them that.

✓ **Validate their concerns.** If it's real to them, it's real. Listen to your team. Let them voice their concerns and don't underestimate the impact these concerns might have on the individual, i.e., their trust in the company, their confidence in their future.

✓ **Be the leader.** Your staff don't like a loss of control. If they sense you don't have control, their anxiety will increase, perhaps disproportionately to the problem. Coach your team through the issue and help them regain control.

✓ **Seize the opportunity.** It's been said that a pessimist complains about the wind, an optimist expects the wind to change and a realist adjusts the sails. Is the wind changing? Look at ways to benefit from the shift and engage your team in adjusting the sails. This keeps the focus on forward action and influence.

Of all the factors that impact the success of your team during a crisis, your visibility is the key, and the greater the stress, the greater the need for you to be visible. Who will forget the iconic images of Winston Churchill walking the streets of London after the blitzkrieg of WWII? Britain's leader made himself visible to the public to demonstrate that despite the terrible situation, he was not going to hide. It inspired confidence in a nation.

Closer to home, I witnessed a remarkable example of leadership in crisis during the collapse of Nortel. My colleague and friend

Desmond Ryan tackled the rumor mill in a brave and proactive fashion. He researched every rumor and news story circulating and, each week, would send them in an e-mail to his team. A follow-up meeting would give the team an opportunity to talk about the rumors face to face. It created some difficult conversations, and no doubt, there were times when Desmond had to confirm some harsh facts. He had some exceptional talent in his department, individuals who could have jumped ship and sought better offers. Their trust in him was so great, though, that they stayed with the organization until the very end.

Be the leader. Be visible. Tell them what you know.

Power Tools

To be a strong leader in a crisis, you need to get out there with your team and stakeholders. When I say this to clients, however, the first question is "What do I say?" Here are some talking points and questions to ask. Remember, you don't need to have the answers, defend an argument or convince anyone of a certain position. Sometimes the best leadership is about really listening.

How many of you have heard the news about (this issue)?

How did you hear about it?

What did you think when you heard?

What do you know for a fact?

What are your assumptions?

Let's lay out the facts here. How do they fit with the assumptions we just talked about? (Do this now, adding any new information you might have.)

Are your concerns based on the facts or the assumptions?

What would be useful next steps here that you could do or we could take together? (This will get people looking forward, feeling engaged and taking control back.)

Let's map out those steps (put on a white board) and think about the opportunities we might have to influence the outcomes.

When would you like to meet next to continue this discussion? If any of you would like to see me one on one, my door is always open.

SIX

Have a Plan, and Have Confidence in the Plan

"Leadership is the capacity to translate vision into reality."

—Warren G. Bennis

YOU'VE PROBABLY HEARD of Les Stroud, Survivorman. His strategies for surviving in the wilderness translate nicely into survival in the corporate jungle. First and foremost, he insists that you've got to have a plan, and you've got to stay positive.

Plans are critical for any leader. We talked earlier about the changing roles you'll have as you work your way up the ladder. Now that you're in a leadership position, setting vision and strategy are fundamental to your job. From this vision and strategy come goals you've set for yourself, your team and the organization.

I've said it before: nature abhors a vacuum. So if you don't have a plan, your staff will go looking for one and, like the rumor mill, they'll follow the direction of anyone who fills the void, whether the directions are sound or not. Don't be left behind like the French revolutionary who said, "There go my people, I must follow them and find out where they are going, for I am their leader." Be the leader; make the plan.

Your plan shouldn't be a secret. Every stakeholder should know what's slated in the short- and long term; otherwise, how can you engage your team in helping you achieve your strategy? You should be able to sketch out your plan at the drop of a hat, in 10 minutes or less, without PowerPoint or other visual aids.

Try not to get locked into the notion of long-term plans. It's great to be looking three to five years into the future, but in an atmosphere of rapid change, those plans likely won't be relevant that far into the future. So be prepared to revisit and alter your plans. Ask for input and flex the plan to adapt to present conditions or unforeseen changes. Your plans won't be chiseled in stone. They'll be carved in wax. Changes will be inevitable, so your plan is simply a guide to follow.

Just as critical as having a plan is staying positive about that plan. This is particularly important during times of crisis. Your positive attitude and confidence in your plans will reassure and calm your team.

I'm not talking about pom-poms and brass bands, though. You don't have to be a cheerleader, but, just as you keep ahead of the rumor mill by sharing whatever information you know, you'll stay ahead of the anxiety that can cripple your team by sharing your confidence in your plan. You don't need to have the immediate solution to every problem that may arise, but you should be able to reassure your team that the temporary setback or upheaval is just that, temporary. This is when the ability to sketch out your plan with clarity and speed will pay off. If panic begins to take hold, you can calmly review the strategy you set and brainstorm ways to get the team back on track.

Be the leader. Be positive. Share your plan.

Power Tools

We all know that no one feels positive all the time. Give yourself a break if you have moments (days) of doubt, keeping in mind that there are times when you can't let that doubt show, especially if there is a crisis at work. Just as Pierre Elliot Trudeau did during his famous walk in the snow, you should take time alone to ponder your doubts and plan your next moves. Here are some tips on how to keep yourself focused on the positive when you need it the most.

✓ **Meditate.** Do so at least three times a day during days of extreme stress, even if you only have a few minutes. If you don't meditate but know some relaxation exercises, they will also work. The key is to find a place of internal calm. This will keep you focused and will renew your energy. The team will see your calm and follow your lead.

✓ **Don't forget about humor!** Read something funny; think of something that amuses you. There are humorous web sites—bookmark them for moments like this. You might want to share some humor with your team. Laughing instantly reduces stress and makes people feel more positive.

✓ **Remember you aren't alone in the world.** Call or meet with a positive friend. Do not meet with someone so you can commiserate. Sharing negative tales makes you feel temporarily better but will make you feel worse in the long run, as you haven't moved forward to take control. Seek out the friend who is optimistic. Her optimism will rub off on you.

✓ **Exercise.** Go to the gym, go for a brisk walk or
go for a run. Whatever you do to burn off steam,
do it every day while under duress. This will turn
off the adrenaline and help you focus and maintain control.

SEVEN

Take Time to Retreat

"Coming together is a beginning. Keeping together is progress. Working together is success."

—Henry Ford

I'VE TALKED ABOUT the fact that as a leader you are responsible for developing vision and strategy for your team, and I'll talk in the next chapter about ways you can keep the clarity you need to stay focused on creating those visions and strategies. Right now, we're going to explore in-depth the four pillars, or components, of effective retreats and the ways they help you convey important concepts to your team, while delivering solid benefits to your organization.

Corporate retreats, as we mentioned in Chapter Two, are an incredibly powerful, versatile tool. But I'm not talking about the old-school retreat: two days of imprisonment in a windowless banquet room, listening to an incessant string of pseudo-inspirational speeches. Corporate conferences have changed over the years, and as a progressive leader, you should embrace that change. So what makes a good retreat?

A good retreat can take many forms, but let's be clear on one point at the outset: taking the staff out for beer and wings on a Friday is *not* considered a retreat. It doesn't have to take on the size and scope of halftime at Super Bowl, but a good program has some basic components that can be adapted to fit your specific needs.

1. Learning & Skills Development

Skilled professionals are highly mobile and ambitious. A solid educational component can attract and retain the kind of employees you want in your organization, particularly if your company relies on creative assets, or intellectual property. Think about offering courses that hone the "soft skills" like:

✓ Conflict resolution

✓ Employee engagement

✓ Time management

Is your company subject to regulatory scrutiny, e.g., health or financial services? Taking an opportunity to review and reinforce standards *en masse* can improve service delivery while creating a culture of consistency throughout the entire organization. This is especially valuable if your company is spread across the country—or the globe—and face-to-face contact isn't possible.

2. Strategy Sessions

It doesn't matter if you have a staff of three or 30. They will benefit from knowing the direction the team and company are headed, and you'll benefit equally from the input and observations you get from them. Spending time discussing strategy gives your staff focus, and it will galvanize that focus when they get back to their offices. They'll have a sense of inclusion because they understand the organization's short- and long-term goals. Ultimately, it will increase loyalty and retention.

3. Team Building & Networking

Education and strategy sessions are certainly important ingredients, but don't underestimate the value of the intangibles, the morale builders. Giving your staff an opportunity to "work" together in a less formal environment allows them to learn about each other and fosters a sense of community.

Be creative; hold the team-building exercises at a variety of venues, from a bowling alley to a bocce pitch. Consider a citywide GPS treasure hunt. If you hold them regularly, the activities in your retreats can be more adventurous as your team becomes more comfortable with the format and more willing to "color outside the lines." Can't get out, or concerned about varying levels of physical fitness on the team? Think about a games night, including video games or do-it-yourself board games, or bring in an outside service.

4. Reflection on Successes

The notion of learning from our mistakes has embedded itself in our corporate culture, but there's much more to be said for learning from our successes and focusing on team or corporate goals. Those of you who play golf (or have ever watched a golf game) know where to align yourself before the swing. You look to the hole and the flag! Why? If you look somewhere else, your body will align in that direction and your shot will be off the mark. Focusing on successes during your retreat will set a positive tone for your staff, casting off any negative events that might have happened earlier in the day, putting them in a good frame of mind. To help your team achieve new heights, set them to the task of describing the things they did that worked. Or, better yet, the things their *colleagues* did that worked. This gives them the opportunity to appreciate the work of another department and provides much-needed recognition for the recipients. Of all the activities your staff can pursue, this one is the cornerstone of retention.

The Bonus Tip:

5. Your Secret Weapon: A Professional Facilitator

Your HR staff might have the time and resources in-house to plan and run your company retreat, but if they don't, then bringing in outside expertise can certainly elevate your game plan.

Facilitators are trained to respond to the specific needs of your company and can manage your entire retreat. They will be:

✓ Neutral gatekeepers, a vital ingredient if you want candid input from all parties during strategy sessions and seminars.

✓ The glue that holds the speakers together.

✓ The "emergency response team" when the unexpected occurs.

✓ The diplomatic timekeepers, ensuring a smooth transition from session to session, keeping the proceedings flowing so that schedules and targets are met.

Professional facilitators can also create an evaluation format and generate reports based on feedback from participants, identifying areas that need further attention and ensuring learning goals have been met. This is a really valuable tool if you plan to hold a series of retreats; it will prevent redundancy and knowledge gaps in future seminars. It's also useful if you're trying to assess the need for ongoing training and want to be sure the exercise was beneficial.

Whether you hold your retreats quarterly, bimonthly, for the whole organization or for individual departments, using this vehicle will net dividends for you, your staff and your company.

Be the leader. Share your vision. Take time to retreat.

Power Tools

Having a great facilitator can make an enormous difference and significantly reduce your stress level. There are
professional facilitator associations in most, if not all,
major cities. Give them a call and ask for a list of facilitators near you. Ask each facilitator:

- ✓ How often she works.

- ✓ How much experience she has.

- ✓ What kind of training she has.

- ✓ Where she has recently facilitated.

Get references and check them! Ask the references
(among other things):

What did this facilitator do best?

What could she have done better?

*What was the evaluation rating among the partici-
pants?*

If you find a facilitator who doesn't do evaluations, I rec-
ommend you don't use him. Follow-up is a key for any
facilitator worth his salt.

You can also ask around as to whom your colleagues have
used. Most of my work comes through word-of-mouth
business.

Don't be afraid to ask a facilitator to visit you and make a
short presentation. Evaluate him based on guidelines such
as these:

✓ Did he show up on time?

✓ Did he ask you questions about what you want to see? (If he doesn't ask you questions now, he might not involve you later.)

✓ Did you like his presentation?

✓ Did you feel energized when he was done?

I'd love to tell you there is a set price that you should or should not pay, but the price varies widely. My prices are different for facilitating a strategy session versus facilitating a retreat versus facilitating a retreat in addition to being a presenter for a couple of workshops at that retreat. Be prepared to pay for quality and outcomes. The more you ask in terms of hours and preparation, the more it costs, but if you are only having two retreats a year, you want to do it right.

EIGHT

Take Time to Reflect

"Clarity affords focus."

—Thomas Leonard

MOST OF THE tips I've discussed so far involve direct interaction with your staff. It's equally important as a leader to remove yourself periodically. Think you don't have the time? If Bill Gates can do it, so can you.

Sure, you probably don't have the luxury of secluding yourself in a beachfront cottage for a Gates-style seven-day "Think Week" with nothing but your books, your laptop and a personal chef, but something on a smaller scale will work just as well.

As the leader, it's your job to develop the visions and strategies that will guide your team in the short- and long term. It will be very difficult to formulate those big-picture visions, though, if you remain immersed in the activity and distractions of the daily show.

It's important that you dedicate one or two hours a month to deliberate reflection. This will afford you the opportunity to not only assess where your company and your team are headed but also to evaluate your own performance based on the targets you've set for yourself.

Whether you remove yourself from the office completely or just remove the potential interruptions from e-mails, phone calls, text messages and visitors, take the time to reflect and ask yourself:

✓ Am I in the right place at the right time for my career, my development, my team's development?

✓ Is my plan still relevant, or does it need to be adjusted?

✓ Am I providing my team with the leadership tools necessary to move the plan forward?

✓ Are my actions aligned to the corporate vision and goals?

On an operational front, you can:

✓ Review your major projects—do you have the resources you need?

✓ Conduct a gap analysis—has anything slipped through the cracks?

✓ Assess your strategies—are they relevant for the current climate, or do you have to readjust?

It's an old saying, but it holds true here—if you can't see the forest for the trees, find the high ground and look down.

Be the leader. Maintain clarity. Take time to think.

Power Tools

Follow these steps to get the most from your self-reflection:

✓ **Seek refuge.** Where do you go when you have to think deeply? Please tell me it's not at the wheel of your car while you're driving! Is there a place you regularly go when you need to gather your thoughts? Even if it's outside, go to that place; you can take your pen and paper or your tablet with you (just be sure to disable your mail program so you aren't distracted by incoming messages).

✓ **Choose your prime time.** When do you have the most energy? Do you get your great ideas in the morning, afternoon or evening? Set aside time to reflect during this part of your day.

✓ **Remove distractions.** Turn off your cell phone and computer and shut the door if you are thinking inside a building. Ask not to be disturbed.

✓ **Keep the right tools at hand.** Are you a big-picture thinker? If so, have a large place to sketch out your ideas. This may be a good time for that write-erasable wall paint or a large whiteboard.

✓ **Now hold still.** A walk or a workout might stimulate your mind, but to give substance and clarity to your thoughts, you will need to reduce all external distractions, like reaching for a towel or monitoring or changing equipment. You might find it very hard to sit still at the beginning. After 15 minutes you will calm down and turn inward. This requires discipline like any other practice, so with time, you will get better at it and will be able to turn the outside world off quite quickly.

NINE

Have Fun!

"Humor is a great thing, the saving thing. The moment it crops up, all our irritation and resentments slip away, and a sunny spirit takes their place."

—Mark Twain

IT'S NOT ROCKET science: laughter makes us feel good, mentally and physically. Is it your job as leader to make your staff feel good?

Absolutely.

I can't tell you how many times I've talked to managers who, when confronted with this fact, respond, "They're just lucky they have a job, it's not *my job* to make them happy!"

Wrong.

Your team reflects your leadership style. So if you simply punch the clock, put in your time, then punch out, your team will mirror that behavior. Work will become that space in which you all just go through the motions, waiting for that "five o'clock world" like in the song from The Vogues. Absent will be the energy that inspires innovation and fuels forward motion.

Don't get me wrong, I'm not suggesting you do a stand-up routine at the water cooler or wear a red nose and make balloon animals at the next staff meeting. Humor comes in many forms and can be shared in a variety of ways that don't require props and punch lines.

Sharing a humorous anecdote, especially something personal, will not only generate good feelings in your staff but will result in better relationships with them. Giving colleagues a lighthearted glimpse into your life outside the office will help your staff see you as an approachable leader and will help everyone (including you) relax.

Be cautious with workplace humor, though. Think *Seinfeld,* not *The Office.* For example, a safe anecdote to share might be along the lines of "I was so focused on this morning's meeting, I drove halfway to work before I realized I hadn't dropped the kids at school!" An unsafe anecdote would begin with "The funniest thing happened to my husband and me at the nude beach this weekend…"

Contemplating sharing a joke or cartoon you found on the Internet but not sure if it's appropriate for your staff? Don't share it. If you have to think about it, don't do it.

Humor is a powerful tool. It reduces stress, fosters feelings of camaraderie. It can ease a tense moment and infuse a meeting with positive energy. Sharing laughter forms bonds among peers just as effectively as any team-building exercise you could undertake with your team.

Be the leader. Lighten up and laugh.

Power Tools

If you are the sort who finds it difficult to think about the office environment as a place where you would have fun, it might be easier to think of it in terms of employee engagement. When people feel positive about an experience, they want to repeat the experience to feel positive again. Fun = Positive.

✓ **Encourage the creation of a team engagement (or fun) committee.** Your staff will lead the charge on creating events that will be fun for them. This won't feel like work for those social types who thrive on this sort of thing. Just being on the committee will be engagement for these individuals. Give them a small budget and let them fly! The events could be anything from a 20-minute mini-putt game through an open space in the office to a bocce ball tournament during the summer once per week for few weeks at lunchtime.

✓ **Bring in the funnies.** Share cartoons or movie clips that strike you as funny; so long as they aren't mean or sarcastic, you should be fine. If in doubt, don't use it. Again, think *Seinfeld*, not *The Office.*

✓ **Go public.** Set up a bulletin board in the kitchen area to post humor. Encourage the team to participate, but be sure to monitor for inappropriate contributions!

✓ **Add a fun event into your retreats.** I often host a trivia game involving guessing the names of musical tunes. This is a great way to finish off a long day of work and really helps everyone to relax and have fun—even you!

TEN

Be Calm

"I start with the premise that the function of leadership is to produce more leaders, not more followers."

—Ralph Nader

I'VE TALKED ABOUT the ways in which your team takes the lead from you: your interactions with technology, your sense of humor, your response in times of crisis. You set the tone, and if you're unable to remain calm in times of stress, it's unlikely that your team will, either.

Workloads have increased during the past 20 years. In the wake of downsizing, rightsizing and reorganizing, there are fewer people doing the same amount of work. Succumbing to the stress is understandable, but not inevitable.

What's at stake if you don't manage workplace stress? Quite a bit. Researchers in Great Britain conducted a thought-provoking study, Whitehall Study II, examining the relationship between work environments and health in the context of their highly stratified social structure. Their findings, while contentious, revealed some interesting insights that can be applied in our backyard.

The British researchers identified a direct link between a perceived lack of control and a greater incidence of heart disease, diabetes and ulcers. Those in relatively junior or support roles (i.e., clerical and janitorial staff) who believed they were stuck in their positions, with no option of advancement, suffered from significantly more stress-related illnesses than those in senior roles. Despite the fact that individuals in higher positions bore greater responsibility than their junior counterparts, they enjoyed better health. It wasn't their workload that dictated quality of life or lack thereof; it was the perception of control over their environment that had the greatest impact. While some have suggested that establishing a sense of control in the British civil service would likely require a thorough realignment of a centuries-old hierarchy, the task should not be so daunting on this side of the pond.

Is your own sense of calm threatened? You may be experiencing physical symptoms: chronic neck pain, back pain or stomachaches, or a sense of defeat that makes you feel despondent towards friends, family and coworkers. You might be using words like "swamped," "impossible," or "relentless" to describe your own workload. Chances are, the stress is overtaking you, and you're most certainly sending the wrong signals to your team.

It's vital that you remain calm and in control, and that you enable your staff to feel that same sense of calm and control.

Be the leader. Stay in control. Stay calm.

Power Tools

In Case of Emergency

Why do hotels and office buildings keep their emergency procedures posted on walls and doorways? Because when an emergency occurs, the occupants need ready access to the instructions they'll need to cope with the crisis, e.g., exit the building safely.

Build your own **Emergency Procedures** list, and keep it close at hand (in a desk drawer, in a specific slot in your briefcase). It should include the following steps:

1. **Take time to breathe.** Find an action that calms you, e.g., a walk around your office building. Allow yourself 5–10 minutes to relax and clear your head.

2. **Make a plan.** Give yourself 15–20 minutes to objectively assess the tasks on your desk and ask yourself these questions:

   • Can I negotiate more time to address the pending issues?

   • Can I delegate some of these tasks to someone else in my department?

   • Can I partner with someone who will bring strengths and skills to streamline the process?

3. **Execute your plan.** Take your plan and run with it.

Get Centered

Have a look back to the tools at the end of Chapters Five and Eight. Many of those tools are critical to the process of staying calm and centered. Here are a few more:

✓ **Check your internal barometer.** Do you feel centered and focused? If not, analyze what's going on to pinpoint the source of anxiety so you can make a plan to deal with it.

✓ **Look at your team.** Do they seem calm? Are they acting calm? If you are calm, they will be calm. If you see them anxious, then you need to dig a little deeper and maintain your composure.

✓ **Take care of yourself.** During stressful times, you need to increase your self-control and monitor your body. Ensure you are eating properly and getting enough sleep and exercise. Decrease your intake of caffeine and alcohol. This is no time to get sick because you haven't been taking care of yourself!

✓ **Take time to relax and have fun with the team,** even if it's only for a few minutes. A bit of laughter goes a long way (see Chapter Nine).

✓ **Stay alert and accessible.** Be more attentive to the team when the pressure is high. They need a calm leader closer than usual when they are stressed (see Chapter Five). You need them to perform well, so create the ideal circumstances for this to occur.

AFTERWORD

"To succeed, one must be creative and persistent."

—John H. Johnson

SO HERE ARE the tips and tools in one place for easy access. All you need now is two very important ingredients: you and your drive. Keep this book close to where you work so as issues come up, you have coaching advice and implementation tools where you need them, when you need them. If you'd like more, give me a call!

Be the leader you admire and enjoy the journey.

RECOMMENDED READING

Blink: The Power of Thinking Without Thinking, Malcolm Gladwell (New York: Little, Brown and Company, 2005)

Death by Meeting: A Leadership Fable...About Solving the Most Painful Problem in Business, Patrick M. Lencioni (San Francisco: Jossey-Bass, 2004)

Leadership Is an Art, Max Dupree (New York: Doubleday, 2004)

Quick Team-Building Activities for Busy Managers: 50 Exercises That Get Results in Just 15 Minutes, Brian Cole Miller (New York: AMACOM, 2004)

Rework, Jason Fried and David Heinemeier Hansson (New York: Random House, 2010)

The First 90 Days: Critical Success Strategies for New Leaders at All Levels, Michael Watkins (Boston: Harvard Business School Press, 2003)

Make Their Day! Employee Recognition That Works: Proven Ways to Boost Morale, Productivity, and Profits, Cindy Ventrice (San Francisco: Berrett-Koehler, 2009)

The Tipping Point: How Little Things Can Make a Big Difference, Malcolm Gladwell (New York: Little, Brown and Company, 2002)

The Whitehall I & II Studies:
www.ncbi.nlm.nih.gov/pubmed/167477;
www.workhealth.org/projects/pwhitew.html;
ije.oxfordjournals.org/content/34/2/251.full

Would you like free reference information and articles to continue your leadership development journey?

Sign up for our free quarterly newsletter at
www.SpearheadExecutiveCoaching.com.

Follow us on Twitter **@SpearheadCoach**
and get links to great leadership articles.

While you're on the web site, check out the exceptional services Spearhead Executive Coaching offers that can move your company to the front of the line:

- Coaching

- 360s

- Workshops

- Retreats

Book Katherine to speak at your next retreat.
She can be reached at
katherinecraig@spearheadexecutivecoaching.com.

CPSIA information can be obtained at www.ICGtesting.com
Printed in the USA
LVOW081950050912

297561LV00001B/1/P